SAMUEL BARBER

CANZONE

for Flute and Piano

G. SCHIRMER, Inc.

DISTRIBUTED BY

HAL•LEONARD®
CORPORATION
7777 W. BLUEMOUND RD. P.O. BOX 13819 MILWAUKEE, WI 53213

to Manfred Ibel
Canzone

Samuel Barber*

sempre legato e con pedale

*Transcribed from the Second Movement of the Piano Concerto, Op. 38.

45311C

to *Manfred Ibel*

Canzone

Flute

Samuel Barber*

45311C

U.S. $7.99

HL50289400

ISBN 978-0-7935-3816-4